# BROKEN WING
## AND
## OTHER POEMS


## BY S.E. MCKENZIE

i

ISBN-10: 1772810150

DEDICATION
To everyone who has been left out in the cold

THIS BOOK IS A BOOK OF SPECULATIVE FICTION
Characters, companies, governments, places, events, are either products of the author's imagination or used fictitiously. Any resemblance to persons (living or dead), companies, governments, places and/or events, is a coincidence and unintentional.

# TABLE OF CONTENTS

# A LEAP

# IN

# THE DARK

# A LEAP IN THE DARK
## I

He closed his eyes
I closed mine too
Together we took a walk in the park;

That was still green;
We gazed into the sky
That was still blue.

We opened our eyes;
There was no space
We just heard slander in our face.

The mob gave us no room to breathe
No room to walk
No room to ride.

The highway crashed through
All we knew
As the watchers

Walked in the middle of the path;
Would give us no room; felt so much doom;
We were belittled by Peasant King's Culture of Obstruction

Kept us pinned
Against the wall;
We felt so small when forced to crawl.

Process to survive was killing us.

Construction of Obstruction;
Life of Destruction
As they built Mega-walls

So high, we could not see

Any of life's Beauty;
We closed our eyes to see
The park and the sky.

Closed eyes can still cry;
We were pinned; left talking to shadows on the wall;
In this cave; there was mandated alienation

Meant to make us feel small;

Stuck in this impoverished Shadow Nation;
They gave us no room
Just to be you and me;

They told us how to live;
They planned how we would die;
Behind the wall without a door;

Stuck in this Shadow Nation;
So many lost what they had before.
Ghettoized behind the wall without a door.

They see our face
And they blow out smoke
To make us choke;

They have money to burn
As we are still waiting
Our turn.

Ghettoized in segregation;
Monopoly of Cronies;
Broken ties with no integration;

Their land is called Paradise where God we trust
Is written on the ticket to get in;
Have enough tickets then your life will begin.

Otherwise
You will stay stuck in this Shadow Nation
Mandated by alienation; they say

We have no other way to enter Paradise
Until we die; we are left in this Shadow World
Which is as cold as ice.

The only world we are connected to;

Is the Shadow-World;
Where so many chained to walls
Can only see and relate

To shadows in the halls;
When light leaps in the dark
We close our eyes to play in the park.

This world without love
Is as cold as hate; to alienate is their mandate;
While water holds a charge;

The spark felt friction
Took a leap in the dark
Just to feel the energy all around

Not letting go was your first mistake;
So Rich so Fake;
Peasant King had so much money to burn

As we were still waiting our turn.

Peasant King used his tickets to pay Beauty
To scratch
Every itch.

We see the mob
On the corner; standing there to intimidate;
To alienate is their mandate; the mob falls

For snob appeal.

## II

Life was not ours to keep
Once we fall into eternal sleep
In Infinity we may still creep;

Life moves on
Into Eternity
No more winners and losers

Trapped within this food chain
That pins us against the wall;
The Process was killing us so we could survive

Mandated Alienation;
Made us feel so small
When forced to crawl

After shadows in the hall.

### III

Rolling Thunder
Light in the sky
Shot at us

And there was no goodbye
As we rolled up
To die;

Peasant King
Had so much money to burn
While we were still waiting our turn

In the dark
We had to leap
To touch the faint light;

The mystery
We were all waiting for
At the end of our war.

Rolled up in sleep
Life inside
Was all that was left for Evermore.

Life leaped into the sky
As we faded away to die
With no time to say goodbye.

Pinned against the wall;
Mandated alienation made us small
Made us crawl.

## IV

So many stigmatized
Then rounded up
Behind the wall

Before the fall
We found the hole
Now not too proud to crawl;

We struggled out of the ghetto
While they threw their garbage over the wall
Turning ghettoes into slums;

So they could then sanitize;
Mandated alienation
So lost in this Shadow Nation;

Their subjective manners;
Justified calling us rude;
Pinned against the wall;

Left to feel so small;
Lost in the slums;
The called us bums.

And how they fought each other
To win the right to apply
For government grants

To bury us
After we died
No one was left to care

When the Peasant King lied.

## THE END

S.E. McKENZIE

# BROKEN WING

# BROKEN WING
## I

Hey Eagle
How did you soar
Into the sky

With your wing
So broken and sore?
You lifted me higher

Than I ever felt before.

Militant old man with hair of straw
He didn't have to
Follow the law;

If he had only wings
Instead of hands
He could have flown all over the lands;

In a fashion so migratory;
Creating a peaceful story;
That is not gory; Like Eagle

Fighting to live.
Militant old man with hair of straw
Might learn to love what he just saw.

Before the big one
Shakes down the earth
Climate change

Deriving fuel
For Hell's fire to burn
While we all know

We will be waiting a long time
For our turn
While space around us is left to burn.

Eagle flew overhead
He flew over those who were dead;
Some were reported missing

And some were not;
The dead were left just there to rot;
Without a care

Watchers weren't there;
For they were watching us;
Creating so much doubt

Hand on the trigger;
Hatred without
Tolerating; shouted out;

And love cried out in pain; needing to give
To live; to feel alive
To survive.

## II

Hey Eagle where do eagles fly
When they are not yet
Ready to die.

Hey Eagle
You came back to me
Your wings almost surrounding me;

Even now when nature once free
Is so fenced in
Involuntarily

By reality so augmented;
Demented;
Future souls so discontented

So many undocumented;
Future's feet so cemented;
Floods and fires

Without known precedent;
Walls that hide the losing side;
Boosts Militant Old Man's pride?

Separation
From the garden
Left fiery footprints

From the other side of Hell.

Hey Eagle, you have so much to tell
You have flown
Above the wall

Separating Heaven and Hell.

Our foe so cruel fed the fire's fuel;
Dogma's rule;
Fell here and there;

But you Eagle did not scare;
You fly so high and above it all;
While we are left down here to crawl

In man's economic misery;
Just an extension from ancient history;
Your domain is the sky and in it you fly
And soar

With one wing so broken and sore.

### III
With a broken wing
Eagle was pulled
By the other

Force so mysterious
Rewards the curious
With new knowledge; renewed life.

As Eagle flew in the sky sometimes blue
Above the Shadow Nation
That he knew

So demented
Reinvented
Disoriented.

## IV

Eagle flew
Into
Destiny

Came back
Stronger than ever before
Learned to fly

With a wing broken and sore.
He flew past threat of extinction
He flew as the symbol of the Nation

hat a sensation
For the disempowered
Generation

Hiding in Demented Shadow Nation

As Eagle's son grew
He never knew
How close he was

To never being
Alive
To nest so close to the sky

History cannot change
Future cemented
Into Demented Shadow Nation

Migratory; Eagle flew
Over every border
Below the sky sometimes blue;

Living his very own story

Looking for prey
Quickly fading away
In Demented Shadow Nation

We were tolerated if we didn't speak;
They watch us as we grew weak;
We had nowhere to take a leak.

Eagle recovered better than us;
For us very few who would give us trust;
Soon we would return to dust.

As Eagle looked on;
So many trees were chopped down
Then gone.

Demented Nation
The young were pushed away
With the future of change

The demented stayed on.
Eagle had birds eye view
Watching humanity lost

Greatest opportunity cost

For Demented Shadow Nation
Walled to separate
Paradise from hell.

Eagle migrated; flying
From season to season
Could see humanity

Without reason; flew past their fate;

## V

Still endangered
Eagle soared in the sky
Flew by

The gulls
The skulls
Eagle flew by

Man driving Cadillac
Eagle species was back
Stronger than ever before

Could now pull himself
Off the floor
With a broken wing; still very sore;

Demented; cemented;
Toxic man gets what he can
In this age of rage

Eagle recovered in numbers
Slowly
Flew over the lowly

Made us feel so alone.

Eagle vowed
To never look back;
On the subtle attack

Of his genome
Black and white
Taking flight

Into the future
Eagle soared;
Mass migration

To flee from his cruel foe;

He flew into tomorrow
And flew by
The man in the Cadillac

Never to look back.

Eagle fought when under attack;
So that he could exist for one more day
Flying away from Demented Shadow Nation;

Eagle would not just survive but thrive.
Beyond mere existence
There was harmony

Power to feel the earth sing;

Eagle soared over the wall
Mass migrator;
He flew where ever he pleased.

For the good of all
Eagle had a birds eye view
And some say he could see it all;

With eyes of the all mighty
In flight;
In fight;

Infinity
Continuity
The power of One

When all things are done.
Eagle
Was having fun.

**THE END**

# THE PROJECTOR MONSTER

S.E. McKENZIE

## THE PROJECTOR MONSTER
### I

If I could only read your mind
What secrets would I find?
Would I uncover?

Private space for a lover;
Not a fighter any more,
Only after we shut the door;

To discover where the treasure might be;

To see beyond the face
To find the Inner Place
Sometimes so deep

You climb into that sleeve;
And find a new dimension
Of make believe.

New-age corridor of Infinity;
Rage; without form
Or norm;

A place
With space
For those who can see beyond a face.

In a throw away world.

## II

She did not say goodbye
For she was not ready to die
Even when she stopped living;

Projector Monster only said good bye
After he lied
Could only be real

When wearing a mask;
Need she ask
How smoke and mirrors;

Swords and daggers
Direct energy;
Select synergy;

Could feed those
Left in this waste land
Under a foreign command

In a land of sand
With very little left to demand;
Even though at one time

There was so much
That was grand.
Completes the task

In a throw away world.

Relativity
New destiny
Free from Bigotry;

New found Equity

Light
Defies
Gravity

In a way, we mere mortals never could;
Just a projection;
Emotion; State of mind.

### III
Someone shot
Someone else;
Projector Monster

Brought up on violent games;
Violent TV shows;
Stares and glares where ever he goes.

The worshipers offer sacrifice to their God
Their enemies' blood
Too proud

To feel lost in a crowd
Where negativity
Justifies barriers to entry;

Speak and you will be accused;
An excuse to abuse
Only way to win

In the Sum Zero Game
They all seek the treasure
And the loser is to blame.

When the treasure cannot be found
For it is still in the ground;
Near the dead soldiers who can't make a sound.

Everywhere
To feel supreme
Barriers

Can make the weak minded scream.

Projector Monster
Just another predator
Condescending

Never bending
Relenting in the dark
While light is freer from Gravity's pull

Than his dark mood;
Feel it brood;
Others so unaware

They have no care
Running with their dog
Pony tails swinging in the air;

Missing all the worlds between here and there.

Nouveau Gestapo
Waves to his Secret Watchers
Of the Shadow State;

S.E. McKENZIE

Will never be free in all this Hate.
How they love to discriminate;
Incriminate; Instigate.

Now lost in an ancient dimension;
Forgotten not so long ago;
The same old state of sorrow

Feeds into tomorrow before tomorrow is even there.

Because the treasure cannot be found;
It is still buried in the ground;
Near the soldiers who can't make a sound.

Could never measure quality;
Quantity of Facts
Flooded the gates; before the acts

Of Devastation
Degradation;
Ghettoes hidden in overpriced urbanization.

Pushed many away until they were out of sight;
Soft light in the night; Gravitation
Pulling; reluctant sensation.

Projecting
Onto others so willing
To be stepped on

From above
They never said goodbye
Before the Projector Monster's rage

Made them dead;
Rage projected from his head;
Environmental influence mixed with dread.

## IV

Wealthy armies abound;
Remains resting in the ground;
Dead warriors can't make a sound.

Once there was so much might;
Glistening in the light;
Majestic sight pulsating all night;

Now remains
Sinking in sand;
Wealthiest armies in the land

Have lost command.
The ones stuck in the lower realm
Cried out for equality;

In a throw away world;

Wondered what they were fighting for;
The treasure would never be found
For it was buried in the ground

The dead soldiers cannot make a sound
Though they all knew;
No one could ever win this war;

For the walls were in the way;

No freedom from those walls
That caused urban decay
No Freedom from those walls

Which marginalize everyday
No growth; just decay;
Causing stakeholder progress to delay

In a throw away world.

## THE END

# NOISE

# NOISE
## I

Noise;
Tool for the Old Boys
Before they die; they lie;

While reaching up to the sky
Malice told us not to cry;
Spite told us not to look at him in the eye;

Revenge was always searching for treasure;
For his pleasure.
Hard to measure when always back at zero.

Old Boys are standing under dark clouds;
Young Boys lie in the ground;
Though their presence lingers all around

Space; forgotten face;
No peace in our world;
Rules power in war;

Abounds more than ever before;
Hanging from the sky
A mysterious force holds it all together

Layered dimensions; vibrating;
Can never be owned.
So close to death

Their hearts are turning to stone
They abandon their young; leave them all alone.
Their thirst for power is built on what they own;

Limits what they have to give;
Even though they are dying to live;
Their ability to electrify is gone.

Power;
Creative and destructive;
Negative and positive;

It can marginalize you
Through manufactured lies
That appear to be true;

They marginalize to monopolize
Power;
While they are withering away.

They hold on to power
With too much might;
Cannot make it right;

While they wait all night
For the morning light
They marginalize to monopolize

While manufacturing powerlessness;

They smile; they trivialize content of character
For at times they have none;
Though if they did, life would have been better for everyone;

They did not know what they had done
While their pollution.
Was blocking out the sun;

No surplus energy to find or give;
Ends so polarized and ready to live;
Charging into realms;

Electrically charged;
Pulsating to stay alive;
So afraid of touching; always wanting to survive;

So afraid of exploding;
And never ready to die
They assumed the other side was doomed;

So they didn't even try
To go beyond
Their sum zero game;

For the old boys
Were always told
Never to cry.

Must stay brave
While they decorate
Their cave

While they insinuated
They felt their hatred grow
Into tomorrow

Hardened them from their sorrow.

## II
Old Boys
Push us aside
To protect their pride

So close to the end of life
They disempower others
For confidence sake

While they are withering away
We thank the dimensions of power
Overhead and in between

And the power we have never seen
Brings to our ears
The noise of the sea

And the courage to stay free.

## III

Sell out
Shake out
Push those with no power out

Act of aggression
Manipulate
Through suggestion

We forget
All blood is red;
We fight for the right

For the power of the day
To rule
In the cruelest way;

Part of the game;
To never remember a name
Unless to blame.

Hypnotize
Criticize
Scrutinize

Euthanize
Charity
But never equality

Call it 'giving back'
But only day old crumbs
Keep their derivatives for their chums;

Another source;
Sometimes to conspire;
Soon to tire;

The shower of fire;
The power was taken
Marginalized into a mistaken

Identity
Reduced to tears;
Controlled by fears

Power of Panic
To crash
While we are pulled by the noise of the sea.

No longer able
To hold up
Against vanity's rage;

Tyranny;
Society values
Without warranty;

Blues were felt
While unjust dues
Were paid

To those with good intentions
But could not bend
Or question

The vibes they were about to send;
Without speaking;
The old boys' bones were creaking

While they were shrieking

Marginalizing
And disempowering
The entire Shadow Nation

We were pulled by the noise of the sea;

While others were pulled back into the cave;
The walls were painted as black as black could be;
No light was to shine; made it hard to see;

While the old boys lived in their palace
We in the Shadow Nation
Could not feel malice

For malice was above our status.

## V

Quality of consciousness
Internal dimension;
Left alone in the building

That was falling;
No longer building;
Just remembering the fallen;

As we spread ashes near meadows still green
We remember what we try to remember
As the seasons come and go
From January to December.

## VI

The lie weaved a web
Deceiving many while they wept;
Evil awoke while others slept.

## THE END

# A COG IN THE MACHINE

# A COG IN THE MACHINE
## I

We are just a cog in the mean Machine;
Driven by our oneness
And powers that cannot be seen.

Conditioned to thrive
We are ruled by the mean Machine's drive;
The Machine needs us to stay alive;

United we are clear sighted

Never to disconnect
We stand erect and tall
Alone we feel so small.

Disconnected

The mean Machine would be broken
For Unity energizes our dream
Creates feelings of self-worth and value; must be true.

Social Bureaucratic and all powerful
The mean Machine when disconnected
Can make you and unseen powers scream;

I am who I am
Not just part of the mean Machine;
Without you I cannot be true

Or be free enough to be just me;

## II

You try to live your dream
But all you hear
Is the mean Machine's scream.

You try;
You cry;
You hear it lie

Every day
Until the day
You die;

You look up into the sky
To see the once living have now gone by,
Without even saying goodbye;

### III

He asked for calm
During the storm
All alone and hungry

So many could not get warm.

He knew what I knew
And you knew too
The mean Machine could never cry

And the mean Machine would never die;
The mean machine would always thrive
As long as it had all of us to drive

And keep it alive.

Technology gets complicated
But what is produced
Is over rated

While we the cogs
Feel out dated
And our value is never stated.

Technology increases the underfed's overkill
Decreases the need for goodwill
Between unseen powers;

Behind the mean Machine
Economic input
Output

Chance to get ahead;
Or starve;
Left for dead;

Pity those left out before the final shout;
The ones who are left out sit on the curb;
Some say they want to disturb;

Nowhere else to go
The mean machine attacks their self-worth;
Leaving their mind troubled in self-doubt

With forgotten words they are not allowed to shout.

**THE END**

# FINAL

# SOLUTION

# FINAL SOLUTION
## I

Back breaking work
Dulled his mind;
Over time; he grew unkind;

Pessimistic; low expectations of peers;
So controlled by his fears
Did not treat others like brothers;

So pessimistic about the world
And those that shared his ground;
He forgot that true life was round.

He grew killer eyes; always wore a disguise;
Only free to be himself when wearing a mask
He does not speak when you ask

Anything at all;
He would rather push you into the abyss
And see you crawl;

Make you feel small
While climbing his wall;
Never treating others as brothers;

For him positive thinking
Only happens
When one is drinking.

His toxic word makes others feel absurd;
Professional pessimist;
He spreads dread across the land.

## II

My True Love was under his command;
For the Bully Master
Was My True Love's Boss;

Bully Master was always cross.
As the years went by
The stress it grew contributed to my loss;

As my True Love's heart
Broke in two;
I felt all that pain as it grew.

## III

Doctor Joe Inc.
Told my True Love to prepare
For death was knocking at our door.

Hand in hand we ran;
Took a plane
And flew away.

Leaving our troubles behind
We saw great beauty
It was our duty

For we were preparing for the end.

## IV

Currency falling;
Privacy stalling;
The dispossessed crawling

In the Abyss
Of the new world order
Of Toxic Man;

As hard as steel; Bully Boss
His objectification conditioned him
Not to feel as he demeaned

With his dull wit;
Low expectations
Never treating others like brothers.

## V

Systematically; many
Fell into the Abyss
And were never missed.

Thought control; engineered content
Without our consent
Many were poisoned with fear

Whenever someone different
Came near.
Cops wearing riot gear

Feeling under threat;
While me and my True Love
Were not ready to die yet.

We heard death knocking at our door
But we were flying to a land
We had never seen before.

Hand in hand
We heard the trumpets blare
But me and my True Love didn't care;

We were flying above
This land we love
While death machines roamed below.

Bully Master was armed to the teeth
Underneath
Our plane there was so much pain.

Not what we had voted for;
We wanted life
Not war.

But the hooded grim reaper
Was knocking at our door.
Carrying an ax; was there to collect Death Tax.

But me and my True Love
Had flown away
Hand in hand

We could not stay
Another day in that toxic land;
While death was knocking at our door

We were heading to a land
We had never seen before
We could see the giant wall below;

The higher it grew
Fear did too;
But we were flying above every cloud

We were now in a space
Where a few were allowed
To be; yes we were almost free.

## VI

Culture manufacturing consent
Of hate
Justification to discriminate

Culture pre-packaged in porn
De-engineered and worn
Unlinked from progress; in a state of distress;

The Empress was in a state of undress;
Bully Master was wearing a frown
For someone had stolen his crown

And would not confess.

Bully Master was losing control
The force of Nature was changing his role.
Born to be a poor son he had never known fun.

Living in a beautiful location
They were all fighting
To own the sensation

Living in Paradise lost
The cost
Changed every day;

Price increases never go away
So many people wish they could stay
Once they found Paradise Lost.

The frown of the Clown
Brought them down
But me and my True Love

Had flown away
To discover what we had missed
While watching so many

Crawling in the abyss;
Dysfunction
Bully Master tried to hide

Dysfunction
Hurts his pride
Dysfunction

Makes him choose a side.
His pessimism takes over;
Watch it spread dread

Across the land
As me and my True Love
Fly overhead

Hand in hand.

Grumpy old men congregate in the cave;
Some cover their age with black hair dye
Others; still not brothers, have hair of straw

And do not try;
So content manufacturing consent
While rewriting the law;

No due diligence needed
As they flex their might;
No concern for another's person's right

While me and my True Love
Were flying
Into the Light.

Bully Master was staring and glaring at you
In the middle of the night;
But me and my True Love

Were holding each other tight.

While the Bully Master
Agreed with the Grim Reaper
That it was

To engineer a climate of fear;
Kept so many
In a state of fight and flight;

More to share
When less people
Are there.

## THE END

Produced by S.E. McKenzie Productions
First Print Edition July 2016

Enquiries: 1(778)992-2453
Mailing Address:
*S. E. McKenzie Productions*
*168 B 5th St.*
*Courtenay, BC*
*V9N 1J4*

Email Address:
messidartha@aol.com

http://www.amazon.com/SarahMcKenzie/e/B00H9RWX48/

www.ingramcontent.com/pod-product-compliance
Lightning Source LLC
Chambersburg PA
CBHW060536030426
42337CB00021B/4298